A fat rat

A fat rat is
on the mat.

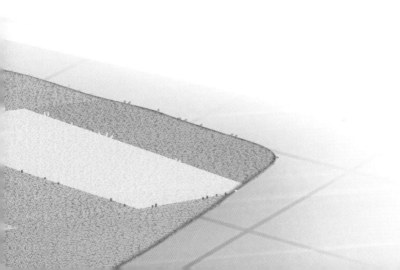

4

Mum runs
to get a net.

Mum lets Sid in.

Sid runs.
The rat runs.

The rat runs
into the gap.

Sid sits and sits.

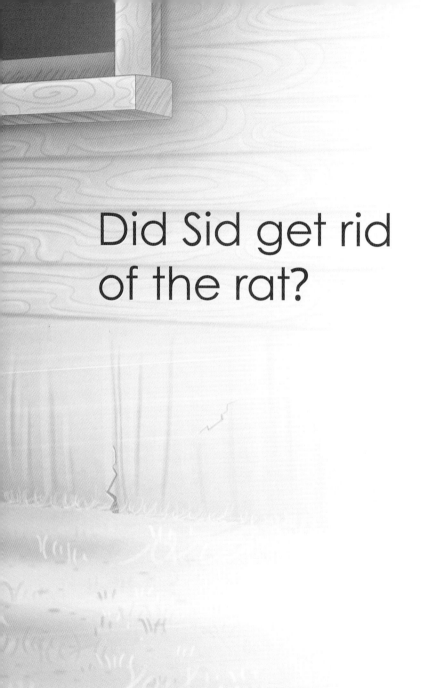

Did Sid get rid
of the rat?

Before reading

Say the sounds: g o b h e r f u l

Ensure the children use the pure sounds for the consonants without the added "uh" sound, e.g. "llll" not "luh".

Practise blending the sounds: rid net rat gap runs sits fat mat lets Sid

High-frequency words: and on Mum did get in **Tricky words:** the of to into is

Vocabulary check: gap – An opening, break or space, e.g. There is a gap in my two front teeth. rid – What does it mean "to get rid of something"? (to remove something)

Story discussion: The title and the cover illustration can give us a good idea about the story. What clues do we have to tell us what this story might be about?

Teaching points: Review the tricky word "into". Remind children that the tricky part is the "o" as it doesn't correspond with the sound /o/ as in "dog". Bring the two words together for children to say. Remind them that "into" is a compound word – it is made from two smaller words as well as being a two-syllable word.

Note that the sound represented for "f" in "of" is /v/.

Review the use of a question mark and an exclamation mark.

After reading

Comprehension:

- Can you retell what happened in this story?
- Did Sid get rid of the rat?
- What would you have done?

Fluency: Speed read the words again from the inside front cover.